My Mystical Year

2022

Name _____

Contact No _____

Email _____

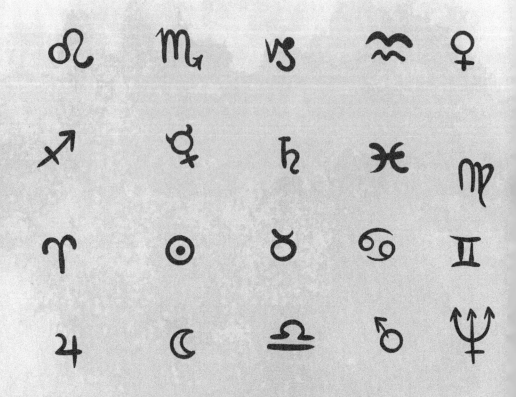

Astrological Glyphs

Dark Moon: Quiet
Inner magic and
meditation

 Waxing Crescent Moon: New
Beginnings
Constructive and Creative

 First Quarter Moon: Attraction
Outwardly Action and
Inspiration

 MOON

 Waxing Gibbous:
Desire
Action and Energy

 PHASES

 Full Moon: All
Purpose
Priorities and Energy

 Waning Gibbous: Cleansing
Closure and Fruition

 Third Quarter Moon: Resolve
Temptations and Overcome
Obstacles

 Waning Crescent Moon: Release
Self Care

Goals for the Year

2022

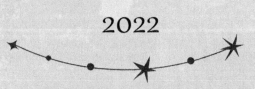

Spiritual Goals		
Goal	Action Steps	Measure of Success

Physical Goals		
Goal	Action Steps	Measure of Success

Goals for the Year

2022

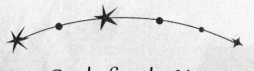
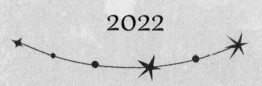

Financial Goals		
Goal	Action Steps	Measure of Success

Improving Good Habits	
Do more of	Do Less of

Chakra Balance

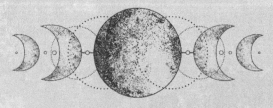

Crown Chakra
Knowledge and Spirituality

Third Eye Chakra
Intuition and Lucidity

Throat Chakra
Communication and Inspiration

Heart Chakra
Acceptance and Sincerity

Chakra Balance

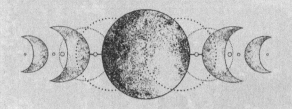

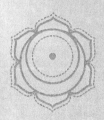

Solar Plexus Chakra
Strength and Determination

Sacral Chakra
Sensuality and sociability

Root Chakra
Energy and Safety

2022

January

M	T	W	T	F	S	S
					1	2
3	4	5	6	7	8	9
10	11	12	13	14	15	16
17	18	19	20	21	22	23
24	25	26	27	28	29	30
31						

February

M	T	W	T	F	S	S
	1	2	3	4	5	6
7	8	9	10	11	12	13
14	15	16	17	18	19	20
21	22	23	24	25	26	27
28						

March

M	T	W	T	F	S	S
	1	2	3	4	5	6
7	8	9	10	11	12	13
14	15	16	17	18	19	20
21	22	23	24	25	26	27
28	29	30	31			

April

M	T	W	T	F	S	S
				1	2	3
4	5	6	7	8	9	10
11	12	13	14	15	16	17
18	19	20	21	22	23	24
25	26	27	28	29	30	

May

M	T	W	T	F	S	S
						1
2	3	4	5	6	7	8
9	10	11	12	13	14	15
16	17	18	19	20	21	22
23	24	25	26	27	28	29
30	31					

June

M	T	W	T	F	S	S
		1	2	3	4	5
6	7	8	9	10	11	12
13	14	15	16	17	18	19
20	21	22	23	24	25	26
27	28	29	30			

July

M	T	W	T	F	S	S
				1	2	3
4	5	6	7	8	9	10
11	12	13	14	15	16	17
18	19	20	21	22	23	24
25	26	27	28	29	30	31

August

M	T	W	T	F	S	S
1	2	3	4	5	6	7
8	9	10	11	12	13	14
15	16	17	18	19	20	21
22	23	24	25	26	27	28
29	30	31				

September

M	T	W	T	F	S	S
			1	2	3	4
5	6	7	8	9	10	11
12	13	14	15	16	17	18
19	20	21	22	23	24	25
26	27	28	29	30		

October

M	T	W	T	F	S	S
					1	2
3	4	5	6	7	8	9
10	11	12	13	14	15	16
17	18	19	20	21	22	23
24	25	26	27	28	29	30
31						

November

M	T	W	T	F	S	S
	1	2	3	4	5	6
7	8	9	10	11	12	13
14	15	16	17	18	19	20
21	22	23	24	25	26	27
28	29	30				

December

M	T	W	T	F	S	S
			1	2	3	4
5	6	7	8	9	10	11
12	13	14	15	16	17	18
19	20	21	22	23	24	25
26	27	28	29	30	31	

2023

January

M	T	W	T	F	S	S
						1
2	3	4	5	6	7	8
9	10	11	12	13	14	15
16	17	18	19	20	21	22
23	24	25	26	27	28	29
30	31					

February

M	T	W	T	F	S	S
		1	2	3	4	5
6	7	8	9	10	11	12
13	14	15	16	17	18	19
20	21	22	23	24	25	26
27	28					

March

M	T	W	T	F	S	S
		1	2	3	4	5
6	7	8	9	10	11	12
13	14	15	16	17	18	19
20	21	22	23	24	25	26
27	28	29	30	31		

April

M	T	W	T	F	S	S
					1	2
3	4	5	6	7	8	9
10	11	12	13	14	15	16
17	18	19	20	21	22	23
24	25	26	27	28	29	30

May

M	T	W	T	F	S	S
1	2	3	4	5	6	7
8	9	10	11	12	13	14
15	16	17	18	19	20	21
22	23	24	25	26	27	28
29	30	31				

June

M	T	W	T	F	S	S
			1	2	3	4
5	6	7	8	9	10	11
12	13	14	15	16	17	18
19	20	21	22	23	24	25
26	27	28	29	30		

July

M	T	W	T	F	S	S
					1	2
3	4	5	6	7	8	9
10	11	12	13	14	15	16
17	18	19	20	21	22	23
24	25	26	27	28	29	30	31

August

M	T	W	T	F	S	S
	1	2	3	4	5	6
7	8	9	10	11	12	13
14	15	16	17	18	19	20
21	22	23	24	25	26	27
28	29	30	31			

September

M	T	W	T	F	S	S
				1	2	3
4	5	6	7	8	9	10
11	12	13	14	15	16	17
18	19	20	21	22	23	24
25	26	27	28	29	30	

October

M	T	W	T	F	S	S
						1
2	3	4	5	6	7	8
9	10	11	12	13	14	15
16	17	18	19	20	21	22
23	24	25	26	27	28	29
30	31					

November

M	T	W	T	F	S	S
		1	2	3	4	5
6	7	8	9	10	11	12
13	14	15	16	17	18	19
20	21	22	23	24	25	26
27	28	29	30			

December

M	T	W	T	F	S	S
				1	2	3
4	5	6	7	8	9	10
11	12	13	14	15	16	17
18	19	20	21	22	23	24
25	26	27	28	29	30	31

Planning Overview

2022

JANUARY

FEBRUARY

MAY

JUNE

SEPTEMBER

OCTOBER

Planning Overview

2022

MARCH

APRIL

JULY

AUGUST

NOVEMBER

DECEMBER

January

Mon	Tue	Wed	Thu	Fri	Sat	Sun
					1	2
3	4	5	6	7	8	9
10	11	12	13	14	15	16
17	18	19	20	21	22	23
24	25	26	27	28	29	30
31						

Notes

February

Mon	Tue	Wed	Thu	Fri	Sat	Sun
	1	2	3	4	5	6
7	8	9	10	11	12	13
14	15	16	17	18	19	20
21	22	23	24	25	26	27
28						

Notes

March

Mon	Tue	Wed	Thu	Fri	Sat	Sun
	1	2	3	4	5	6
7	8	9	10	11	12	13
14	15	16	17	18	19	20
21	22	23	24	25	26	27
28	29	30	31			

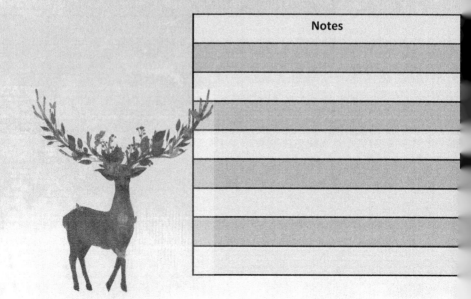

Notes

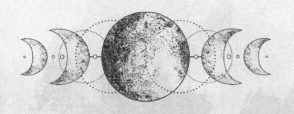

April

Mon	Tue	Wed	Thu	Fri	Sat	Sun
				1	2	3
4	5	6	7	8	9	10
11	12	13	14	15	16	17
18	19	20	21	22	23	24
25	26	27	28	29	30	

Notes

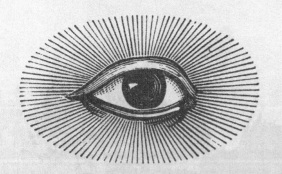

May

Mon	Tue	Wed	Thu	Fri	Sat	Sun
						1
2	3	4	5	6	7	8
9	10	11	12	13	14	15
16	17	18	19	20	21	22
23	24	25	26	27	28	29
30	31					

Notes

June

Mon	Tue	Wed	Thu	Fri	Sat	Sun
		1	2	3	4	5
6	7	8	9	10	11	12
13	14	15	16	17	18	19
20	21	22	23	24	25	26
27	28	29	30			

Notes

July

Mon	Tue	Wed	Thu	Fri	Sat	Sun
				1	2	3
4	5	6	7	8	9	10
11	12	13	14	15	16	17
18	19	20	21	22	23	24
25	26	27	28	29	30	31

Notes

August

Mon	Tue	Wed	Thu	Fri	Sat	Sun
1	2	3	4	5	6	7
8	9	10	11	12	13	14
15	16	17	18	19	20	21
22	23	24	25	26	27	28
29	30	31				

Notes

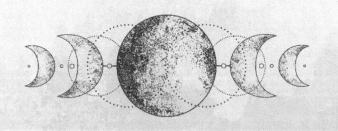

September

Mon	Tue	Wed	Thu	Fri	Sat	Sun
			1	2	3	4
5	6	7	8	9	10	11
12	13	14	15	16	17	18
19	20	21	22	23	24	25
26	27	28	29	30		

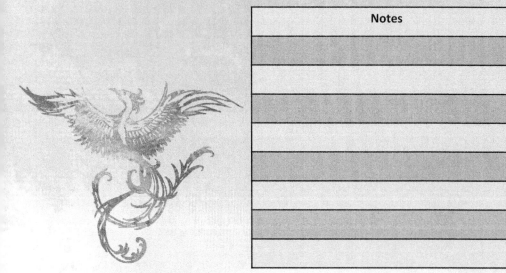

Notes

October

Mon	Tue	Wed	Thu	Fri	Sat	Sun
					1	2
3	4	5	6	7	8	9
10	11	12	13	14	15	16
17	18	19	20	21	22	23
24	25	26	27	28	29	30
31						

Notes

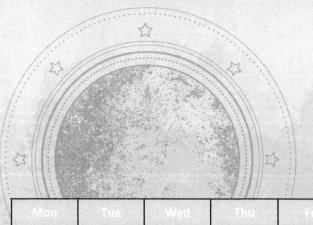

November

Mon	Tue	Wed	Thu	Fri	Sat	Sun
	1	2	3	4	5	6
7	8	9	10	11	12	13
14	15	16	17	18	19	20
21	22	23	24	25	26	27
28	29	30				

Notes

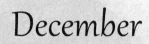

December

Mon	Tue	Wed	Thu	Fri	Sat	Sun
			1	2	3	4
5	6	7	8	9	10	11
13	14	15	16	17	18	19
20	21	22	23	24	25	26
27	28	29	30	31		

Notes

JANUARY
2022

SUNDAY	MONDAY	TUESDAY	WEDNESDAY
2	3	4	5
9	10	11	12
16	17	18	19
23	24	25	26
30	31		

JANUARY

2022

THURSDAY	FRIDAY	SATURDAY	NOTES
		1	
6	7	8	
13	14	15	
20	21	22	
27	28	29	

12/27/21 – 01/02/22

Plans
❏ 27. MONDAY
❏ 28. TUESDAY
❏ 29. WEDNESDAY
❏ 30. THURSDAY
❏ 31. FRIDAY
❏ 1. SATURDAY
❏ 2. SUNDAY

Must be done this week

If I have time

Calls and emails

Notes

January

01/03/22 – 01/09/22

Plans	Must be done this week
☐ 3. MONDAY	
☐ 4. TUESDAY	**If I have time**
☐ 5. WEDNESDAY	**Calls and emails**
☐ 6. THURSDAY	
☐ 7. FRIDAY	**Notes**
☐ 8. SATURDAY	
☐ 9. SUNDAY	

01/10/22 – 01/16/22

January

Plans

☐ 10. MONDAY

☐ 11. TUESDAY

☐ 12. WEDNESDAY

☐ 13. THURSDAY

☐ 14. FRIDAY

☐ 15. SATURDAY

☐ 16. SUNDAY

Must be done this week

If I have time

Calls and emails

Notes

Week 3

January

01/17/22 – 01/23/22

Plans	Must be done this week
☐ 17. MONDAY	
	If I have time
☐ 18. TUESDAY	
☐ 19. WEDNESDAY	**Calls and emails**
☐ 20. THURSDAY	
☐ 21. FRIDAY	
☐ 22. SATURDAY	**Notes**
☐ 23. SUNDAY	

Plans	Must be done this week

01/24/22 – 01/30/22

January

Plans
❑ 24. MONDAY
❑ 25. TUESDAY
❑ 26. WEDNESDAY
❑ 27. THURSDAY
❑ 28. FRIDAY
❑ 29. SATURDAY
❑ 30. SUNDAY

Must be done this week

If I have time

Calls and emails

Notes

Notes

FEBRUARY

2022

SUNDAY	MONDAY	TUESDAY	WEDNESDAY
		1	2
6	7	8	9
13	14	15	16
20	21	22	23
27	28		

FEBRUARY

2022

THURSDAY	FRIDAY	SATURDAY	NOTES
3	4	5	
10	11	12	
17	18	19	
24	25	26	

February

01/31/22 – 02/06/22

Plans	Must be done this week
☐ 31. MONDAY	
☐ 1. TUESDAY	**If I have time**
☐ 2. WEDNESDAY	**Calls and emails**
☐ 3. THURSDAY	
☐ 4. FRIDAY	**Notes**
☐ 5. SATURDAY	
☐ 6. SUNDAY	

02/07/22 – 02/13/22

Plans	Must be done this week
☐ 7. MONDAY	
	If I have time
☐ 8. TUESDAY	
☐ 9.WEDNESDAY	
	Calls and emails
☐ 10. THURSDAY	
☐ 11. FRIDAY	
	Notes
☐ 12. SATURDAY	
☐ 13. SUNDAY	

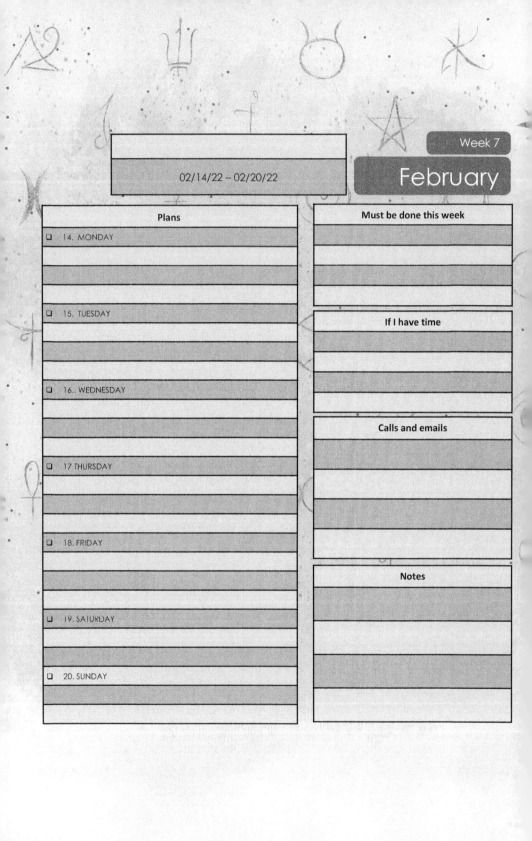

02/14/22 – 02/20/22

February

Plans

☐ 14. MONDAY

☐ 15. TUESDAY

☐ 16.. WEDNESDAY

☐ 17 THURSDAY

☐ 18. FRIDAY

☐ 19. SATURDAY

☐ 20. SUNDAY

Must be done this week

If I have time

Calls and emails

Notes

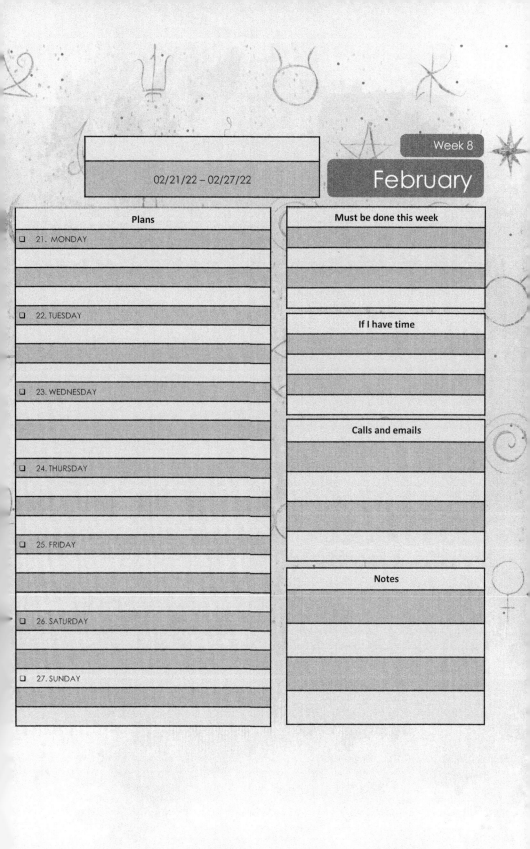

02/21/22 – 02/27/22

Plans

☐ 21. MONDAY

☐ 22. TUESDAY

☐ 23. WEDNESDAY

☐ 24. THURSDAY

☐ 25. FRIDAY

☐ 26. SATURDAY

☐ 27. SUNDAY

Must be done this week

If I have time

Calls and emails

Notes

MARCH

2022

SUNDAY	MONDAY	TUESDAY	WEDNESDAY
		1	2
6	7	8	9
13	14	15	16
20	21	22	23
27	28	29	30

MARCH

2022

THURSDAY	FRIDAY	SATURDAY	NOTES
3	4	5	
10	11	12	
17	18	19	
24	25	26	
31			

March

02/28/22 – 03/06/22

Plans	Must be done this week
☐ 28. MONDAY	
☐ 29. TUESDAY	**If I have time**
☐ 30.WEDNESDAY	
	Calls and emails
☐ 31.THURSDAY	
☐ 1. FRIDAY	
	Notes
☐ 2.. SATURDAY	
☐ 3. SUNDAY	

03/07/22 – 03/13/22

March

Plans
❑ 7. MONDAY
❑ 8. TUESDAY
❑ 9. WEDNESDAY
❑ 10. THURSDAY
❑ 11. FRIDAY
❑ 12. SATURDAY
❑ 13. SUNDAY

Must be done this week

If I have time

Calls and emails

Notes

03/14/22 – 03/20/22

Plans
☐ 14 MONDAY
☐ 15. TUESDAY
☐ 16. WEDNESDAY
☐ 17. THURSDAY
☐ 18. FRIDAY
☐ 19. SATURDAY
☐ 20. SUNDAY

Must be done this week

If I have time

Calls and emails

Notes

03/21/22 – 03/27/22

Plans
☐ 21 MONDAY
☐ 22. TUESDAY
☐ 23. WEDNESDAY
☐ 24. THURSDAY
☐ 25. FRIDAY
☐ 26. SATURDAY
☐ 27. SUNDAY

Must be done this week

If I have time

Calls and emails

Notes

03/28/22 – 04/03/22

Plans
☐ 28. MONDAY
☐ 29. TUESDAY
☐ 30. WEDNESDAY
☐ 31. THURSDAY
☐ 1. FRIDAY
☐ 2. SATURDAY
☐ 3. SUNDAY

Must be done this week

If I have time

Calls and emails

Notes

Notes

_____

_____

_____

_____

_____

_____

_____

_____

_____

_____

_____

_____

_____

_____

_____

_____

_____

APRIL

2022

SUNDAY	MONDAY	TUESDAY	WEDNESDAY
3	4	5	6
10	11	12	13
17 Easter hunt market	18	19	20 Alex Shaele sleepover
24	25	26	27

APRIL

2022

THURSDAY	FRIDAY	SATURDAY	NOTES
	1	2	• Get Mum to reply to Aleks sleepover
7	8	9	
14	15	16	
21	22	23	
28	29	30	

04/04/22 – 10/04/22

Plans
☐   4. MONDAY
☐   5. TUESDAY
☐   6. WEDNESDAY
☐   7. THURSDAY
☐   8. FRIDAY
☐   9.. SATURDAY
☐   10. SUNDAY

Must be done this week

If I have time

Calls and emails

Notes

04/11/22 – 04/17/22

April

Plans

☐ 11. MONDAY

☐ 12. TUESDAY

☐ 13. WEDNESDAY

☐ 14. THURSDAY

☐ 15. FRIDAY

☐ 16. SATURDAY

☐ 17. SUNDAY

Must be done this week

If I have time

Calls and emails

Notes

| 04/18/22 – 04/24/22 | April |

Plans	Must be done this week
☐ 18. MONDAY	
☐ 19. TUESDAY	If I have time
☐ 20. WEDNESDAY	
	Calls and emails
☐ 21. THURSDAY	
☐ 22. FRIDAY	
	Notes
☐ 23. SATURDAY	
☐ 24. SUNDAY	

04/25/22 – 05/01/22

Plans
☐ 25. MONDAY
☐ 26. TUESDAY
☐ 27. WEDNESDAY
☐ 28. THURSDAY
☐ 29. FRIDAY
☐ 30. SATURDAY
☐ 1. SUNDAY

Must be done this week

If I have time

Calls and emails

Notes

MAY

2022

SUNDAY	MONDAY	TUESDAY	WEDNESDAY
1	2	3	4
8	9	10	11
15	16	17	18
22	23	24	25
29	30	31	

MAY

2022

THURSDAY	FRIDAY	SATURDAY	NOTES
5	6	7	
12	13	14	
19	20	21	
26	27	28	

May

05/02/22 – 05/08/22

Plans

☐ 2. MONDAY

☐ 3. TUESDAY

☐ 4. WEDNESDAY

☐ 5. THURSDAY

☐ 6. FRIDAY

☐ 7. SATURDAY

☐ 8. SUNDAY

Must be done this week

If I have time

Calls and emails

Notes

May

05/09/22 – 05/15/22	

Plans

☐ 9. MONDAY

☐ 10. TUESDAY

☐ 11. WEDNESDAY

☐ 12. THURSDAY

☐ 13. FRIDAY

☐ 14. SATURDAY

☐ 15. SUNDAY

Must be done this week

If I have time

Calls and emails

Notes

05/16/22 – 05/22/22

Plans	Must be done this week
☐ 16. MONDAY	
☐ 17. TUESDAY	**If I have time**
☐ 18. WEDNESDAY	
☐ 19. THURSDAY	**Calls and emails**
☐ 20. FRIDAY	
☐ 21. SATURDAY	**Notes**
☐ 22. SUNDAY	

	Week 21
05/23/22 – 05/29/22	May

Plans
☐ 23. MONDAY
☐ 24. TUESDAY
☐ 25. WEDNESDAY
☐ 26. THURSDAY
☐ 27. FRIDAY
☐ 28. SATURDAY
☐ 29. SUNDAY

Must be done this week

If I have time

Calls and emails

Notes

May

05/30/22 – 06/05/22

Plans
☐ 30. MONDAY
☐ 31. TUESDAY
☐ 1. WEDNESDAY
☐ 2. THURSDAY
☐ 3. FRIDAY
☐ 4. SATURDAY
☐ 5. SUNDAY

Must be done this week

If I have time

Calls and emails

Notes

Notes

JUNE

2022

SUNDAY	MONDAY	TUESDAY	WEDNESDAY
			1
5	6	7	8
12	13	14	15
19	20	21	22
26	27	28	29

JUNE

2022

THURSDAY	FRIDAY	SATURDAY	NOTES
2	3	4	
9	10	11	
16	17	18	
23	24	25	
30			

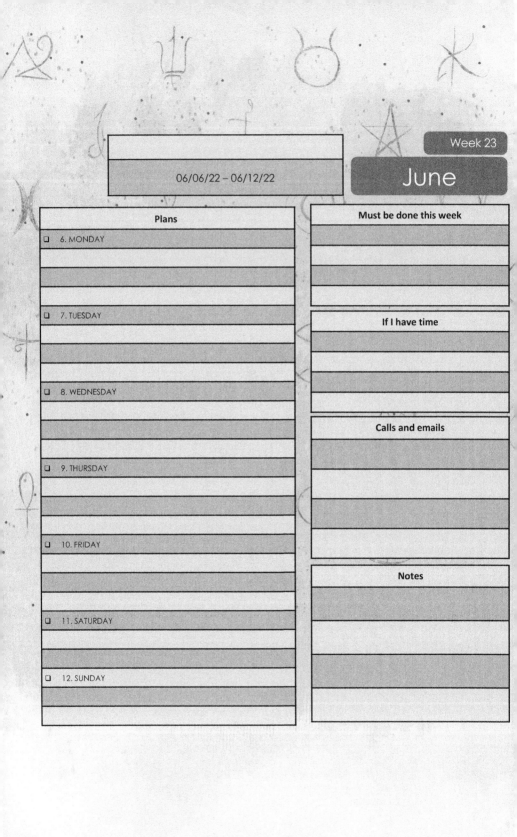

June

06/06/22 – 06/12/22

Plans

☐ 6. MONDAY

☐ 7. TUESDAY

☐ 8. WEDNESDAY

☐ 9. THURSDAY

☐ 10. FRIDAY

☐ 11. SATURDAY

☐ 12. SUNDAY

Must be done this week

If I have time

Calls and emails

Notes

June

06/13/22 – 06/19/22

Plans

☐ 13. MONDAY

☐ 14. TUESDAY

☐ 15. WEDNESDAY

☐ 16. THURSDAY

☐ 17. FRIDAY

☐ 18. SATURDAY

☐ 19. SUNDAY

Must be done this week

If I have time

Calls and emails

Notes

June

06/20/22 – 06/26/22

Plans
☐ 20. MONDAY
☐ 21. TUESDAY
☐ 22. WEDNESDAY
☐ 23. THURSDAY
☐ 24. FRIDAY
☐ 25. SATURDAY
☐ 26. SUNDAY

Must be done this week

If I have time

Calls and emails

Notes

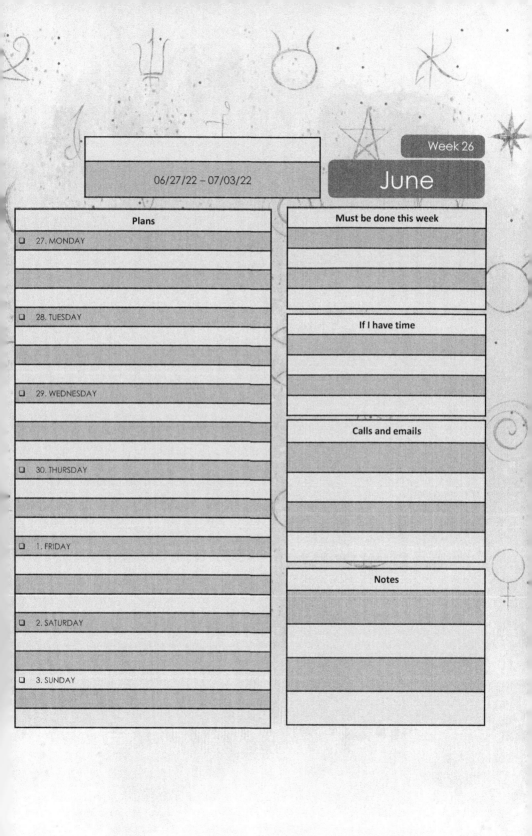

Week 26

June

06/27/22 – 07/03/22

Plans
☐ 27. MONDAY
☐ 28. TUESDAY
☐ 29. WEDNESDAY
☐ 30. THURSDAY
☐ 1. FRIDAY
☐ 2. SATURDAY
☐ 3. SUNDAY

Must be done this week

If I have time

Calls and emails

Notes

JULY

2022

SUNDAY	MONDAY	TUESDAY	WEDNESDAY
3	4	5	6
10	11	12	13
17	18	19	20
24	25	26	27
31			

JULY

2022

THURSDAY	FRIDAY	SATURDAY	NOTES
	1	2	
7	8	9	
14	15	16	
21	22	23	
28	29	30	

JULY

07/04/22 – 07/10/22

Plans	Must be done this week
☐ 4. MONDAY	
☐ 5. TUESDAY	**If I have time**
☐ 6. WEDNESDAY	
	Calls and emails
☐ 7. THURSDAY	
☐ 8. FRIDAY	
	Notes
☐ 9. SATURDAY	
☐ 10. SUNDAY	

07/11/22 – 07/17/22

Plans

- [ ] 11. MONDAY

- [ ] 12. TUESDAY

- [ ] 13. WEDNESDAY

- [ ] 14. THURSDAY

- [ ] 15. FRIDAY

- [ ] 16. SATURDAY

- [ ] 17. SUNDAY

Must be done this week

If I have time

Calls and emails

Notes

07/18/22 – 07/24/22

Plans
☐ 18. MONDAY
☐ 19. TUESDAY
☐ 20. WEDNESDAY
☐ 21. THURSDAY
☐ 22. FRIDAY
☐ 23. SATURDAY
☐ 24. SUNDAY

Must be done this week

If I have time

Calls and emails

Notes

07/25/22 – 07/31/22

July

Plans
☐ 25. MONDAY
☐ 26. TUESDAY
☐ 27. WEDNESDAY
☐ 28. THURSDAY
☐ 29. FRIDAY
☐ 30. SATURDAY
☐ 31. SUNDAY

Must be done this week

If I have time

Calls and emails

Notes

AUGUST

2022

SUNDAY	MONDAY	TUESDAY	WEDNESDAY
	1	2	3
7	8	9	10
14	15	16	17
21	22	23	24
28	29	30	31

AUGUST

2022

THURSDAY	FRIDAY	SATURDAY	NOTES
4	5	6	
11	12	13	
18	19	20	
25	26	27	

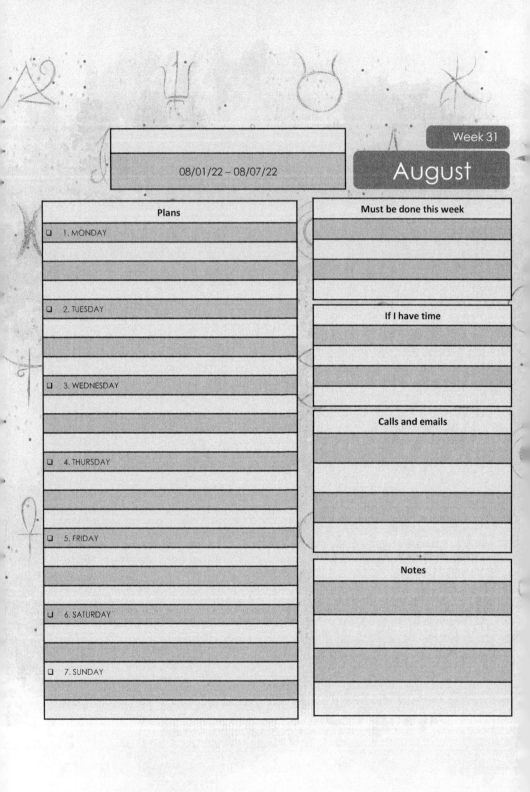

08/01/22 – 08/07/22

August

Plans

- ☐ 1. MONDAY
- ☐ 2. TUESDAY
- ☐ 3. WEDNESDAY
- ☐ 4. THURSDAY
- ☐ 5. FRIDAY
- ☐ 6. SATURDAY
- ☐ 7. SUNDAY

Must be done this week

If I have time

Calls and emails

Notes

	08/08/22 – 08/14/22

Week 32

August

Plans
☐ 8. MONDAY
☐ 9. TUESDAY
☐ 10. WEDNESDAY
☐ 11. THURSDAY
☐ 12. FRIDAY
☐ 13. SATURDAY
☐ 14. SUNDAY

Must be done this week

If I have time

Calls and emails

Notes

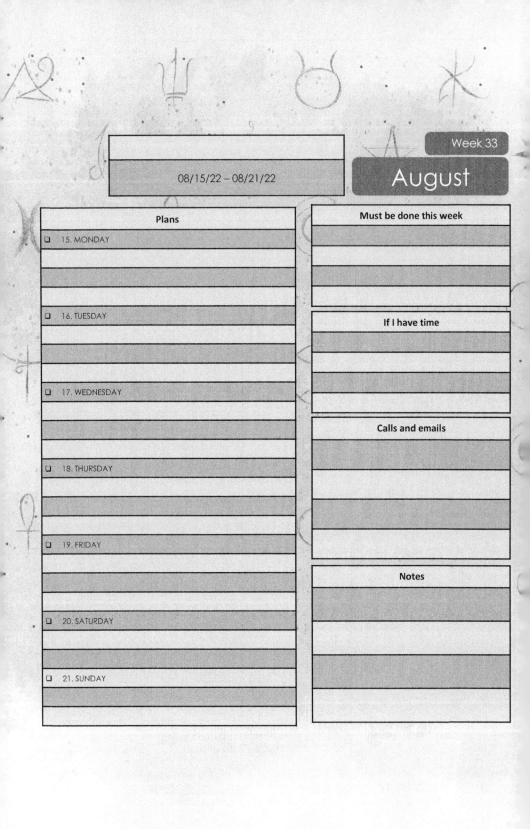

Week 33

August

08/15/22 – 08/21/22

Plans

☐ 15. MONDAY

☐ 16. TUESDAY

☐ 17. WEDNESDAY

☐ 18. THURSDAY

☐ 19. FRIDAY

☐ 20. SATURDAY

☐ 21. SUNDAY

Must be done this week

If I have time

Calls and emails

Notes

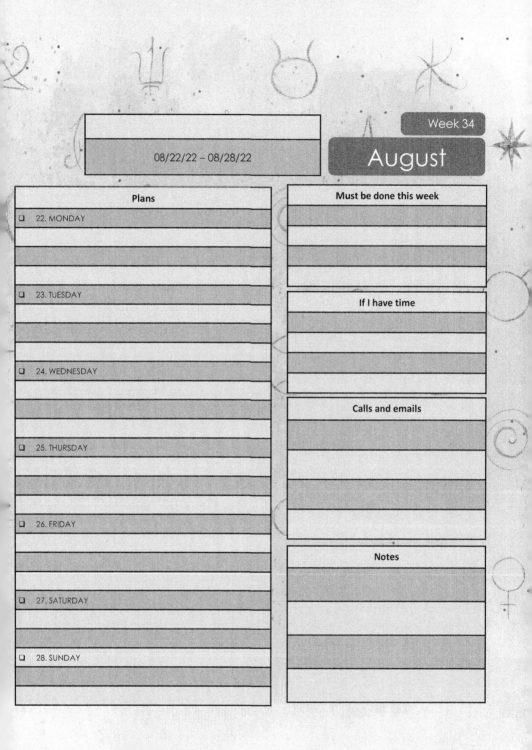

Week 34

08/22/22 – 08/28/22

August

Plans

☐ 22. MONDAY

☐ 23. TUESDAY

☐ 24. WEDNESDAY

☐ 25. THURSDAY

☐ 26. FRIDAY

☐ 27. SATURDAY

☐ 28. SUNDAY

Must be done this week

If I have time

Calls and emails

Notes

08/29/22 – 09/04/22

August

Plans

- [ ] 29. MONDAY

- [ ] 30. TUESDAY

- [ ] 31. WEDNESDAY

- [ ] 1. THURSDAY

- [ ] 2. FRIDAY

- [ ] 3. SATURDAY

- [ ] 4. SUNDAY

Must be done this week

If I have time

Calls and emails

Notes

Notes

_____

_____

_____

_____

_____

_____

_____

_____

_____

_____

_____

_____

_____

_____

_____

_____

SEPTEMBER

2022

SUNDAY	MONDAY	TUESDAY	WEDNESDAY
4	5	6	7
11	12	13	14
18	19	20	21
25	26	27	28

SEPTEMBER

2022

THURSDAY	FRIDAY	SATURDAY	NOTES
1	2	3	
8	9	10	
15	16	17	
22	23	24	
29	30		

September

09/05/22 – 09/11/22

Plans
☐ 5. MONDAY
☐ 6. TUESDAY
☐ 7. WEDNESDAY
☐ 8. THURSDAY
☐ 9. FRIDAY
☐ 10. SATURDAY
☐ 11. SUNDAY

Must be done this week

If I have time

Calls and emails

Notes

09/12/22 – 09/18/22

Plans	Must be done this week
☐ 12. MONDAY	
☐ 13. TUESDAY	**If I have time**
☐ 14. WEDNESDAY	
	Calls and emails
☐ 15. THURSDAY	
☐ 16. FRIDAY	
	Notes
☐ 17. SATURDAY	
☐ 18. SUNDAY	

September

09/19/22 – 09/25/22

Plans
☐ 19. MONDAY
☐ 20. TUESDAY
☐ 21. WEDNESDAY
☐ 22. THURSDAY
☐ 23. FRIDAY
☐ 24. SATURDAY
☐ 25. SUNDAY

Must be done this week

If I have time

Calls and emails

Notes

September

09/26/22 – 10/02/22

Plans

☐ 26. MONDAY

☐ 27. TUESDAY

☐ 28. WEDNESDAY

☐ 29. THURSDAY

☐ 30. FRIDAY

☐ 1. SATURDAY

☐ 2. SUNDAY

Must be done this week

If I have time

Calls and emails

Notes

OCTOBER

SUNDAY	MONDAY	TUESDAY	WEDNESDAY
2	3	4	5
9	10	11	12
16	17	18	19
23	24	25	26
30	31		

OCTOBER

2022

THURSDAY	FRIDAY	SATURDAY	NOTES
		1	
6	7	8	
13	14	15	
20	21	22	
27	28	29	

10/03/22 – 10/09/22

Plans

☐ 3. MONDAY

☐ 4. TUESDAY

☐ 5. WEDNESDAY

☐ 6. THURSDAY

☐ 7. FRIDAY

☐ 8. SATURDAY

☐ 9. SUNDAY

Must be done this week

If I have time

Calls and emails

Notes

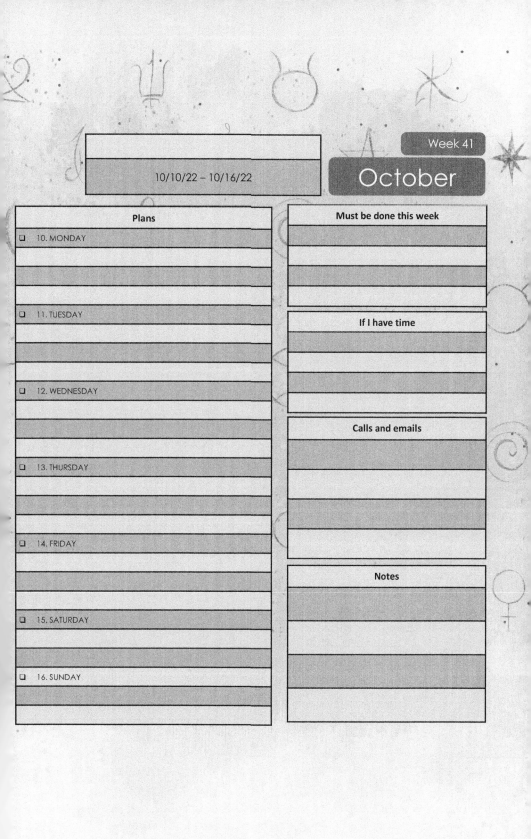

10/10/22 – 10/16/22

Plans

☐ 10. MONDAY

☐ 11. TUESDAY

☐ 12. WEDNESDAY

☐ 13. THURSDAY

☐ 14. FRIDAY

☐ 15. SATURDAY

☐ 16. SUNDAY

Must be done this week

If I have time

Calls and emails

Notes

October

10/17/21 – 10/23/21

Plans
☐ 17. MONDAY
☐ 18. TUESDAY
☐ 19. WEDNESDAY
☐ 20. THURSDAY
☐ 21. FRIDAY
☐ 22. SATURDAY
☐ 23. SUNDAY

Must be done this week

If I have time

Calls and emails

Notes

10/24/22 – 10/30/22

October

Plans

☐ 24. MONDAY

☐ 25. TUESDAY

☐ 26. WEDNESDAY

☐ 27. THURSDAY

☐ 28. FRIDAY

☐ 29. SATURDAY

☐ 30. SUNDAY

Must be done this week

If I have time

Calls and emails

Notes

NOVEMBER

2022

SUNDAY	MONDAY	TUESDAY	WEDNESDAY
		1	2
6	7	8	9
13	14	15	16
20	21	22	23
27	28	29	30

NOVEMBER

2022

THURSDAY	FRIDAY	SATURDAY	NOTES
3	4	5	
10	11	12	
17	18	19	
24	25	26	

November

10/31/22 – 11/06/22

Plans
☐ 31. MONDAY
☐ 1. TUESDAY
☐ 2. WEDNESDAY
☐ 3. THURSDAY
☐ 4. FRIDAY
☐ 5. SATURDAY
☐ 6. SUNDAY

Must be done this week

If I have time

Calls and emails

Notes

November

11/07/21 – 11/13/21

Plans
☐ 7. MONDAY
☐ 8. TUESDAY
☐ 9. WEDNESDAY
☐ 10. THURSDAY
☐ 11. FRIDAY
☐ 12. SATURDAY
☐ 13. SUNDAY

Must be done this week

If I have time

Calls and emails

Notes

11/14/22 – 11/20/22

Plans
☐ 14. MONDAY
☐ 15. TUESDAY
☐ 16. WEDNESDAY
☐ 17. THURSDAY
☐ 18. FRIDAY
☐ 19. SATURDAY
☐ 20. SUNDAY

Must be done this week

If I have time

Calls and emails

Notes

November

11/21/22 – 11/27/22

Plans	Must be done this week
☐ 21 .MONDAY	
	If I have time
☐ 22. TUESDAY	
☐ 23. WEDNESDAY	**Calls and emails**
☐ 24. THURSDAY	
☐ 25. FRIDAY	**Notes**
☐ 26. SATURDAY	
☐ 27. SUNDAY	

11/28/22 – 12/04/22

Plans

☐ 28 MONDAY

☐ 29.TUESDAY

☐ 30. WEDNESDAY

☐ 1. THURSDAY

☐ 2. FRIDAY

☐ 3. SATURDAY

☐ 4. SUNDAY

Must be done this week

If I have time

Calls and emails

Notes

Notes

DECEMBER

2022

SUNDAY	MONDAY	TUESDAY	WEDNESDAY
4	5	6	7
11	12	13	14
18	19	20	21
25	26	27	28

DECEMBER
2022

THURSDAY	FRIDAY	SATURDAY	NOTES
1	2	3	
8	9	10	
15	16	17	
22	23	24	
29	30	31	

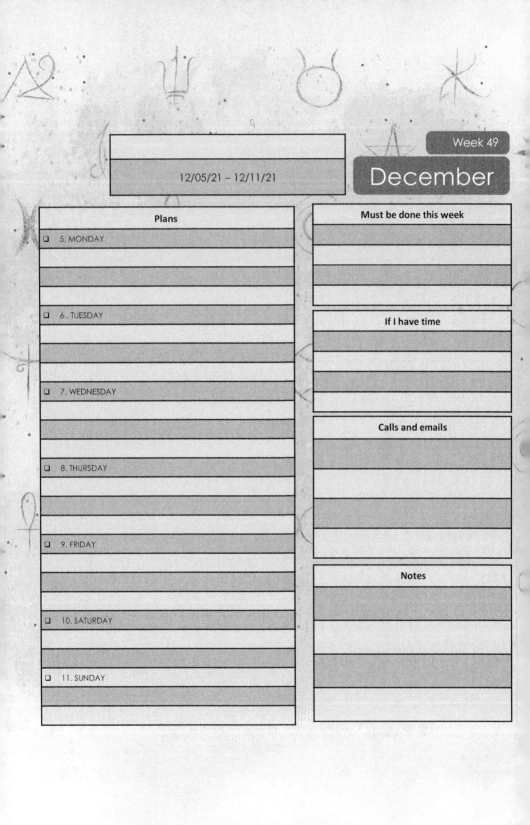

12/05/21 – 12/11/21

Plans

☐   5, MONDAY

☐   6.. TUESDAY

☐   7. WEDNESDAY

☐   8. THURSDAY

☐   9. FRIDAY

☐   10. SATURDAY

☐   11. SUNDAY

Must be done this week

If I have time

Calls and emails

Notes

December

12/12/22 – 12/18/22

Plans

☐ 12. MONDAY

☐ 13. TUESDAY

☐ 14. WEDNESDAY

☐ 15. THURSDAY

☐ 16. FRIDAY

☐ 17. SATURDAY

☐ 18. SUNDAY

Must be done this week

If I have time

Calls and emails

Notes

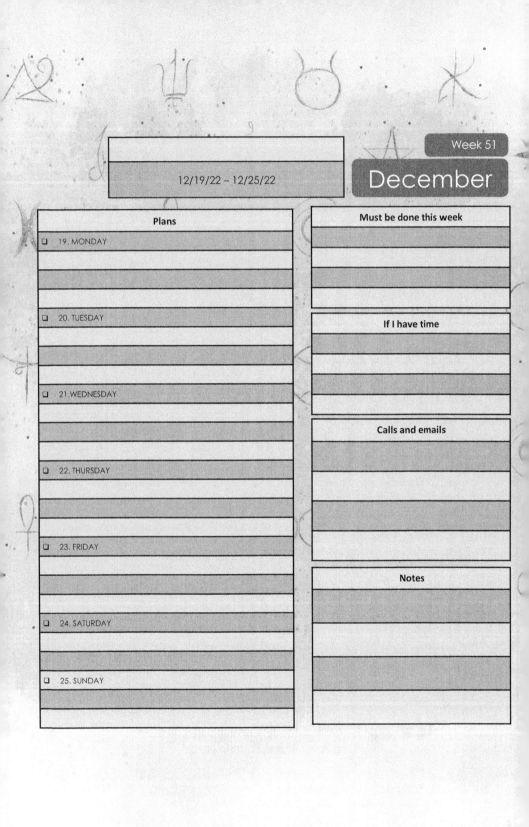

12/19/22 – 12/25/22

Plans
☐ 19. MONDAY
☐ 20. TUESDAY
☐ 21. WEDNESDAY
☐ 22. THURSDAY
☐ 23. FRIDAY
☐ 24. SATURDAY
☐ 25. SUNDAY

Must be done this week

If I have time

Calls and emails

Notes

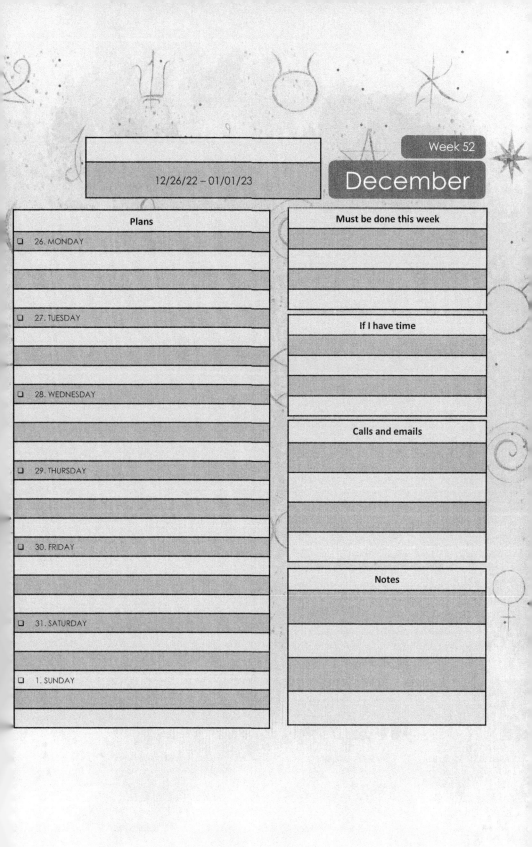

December

12/26/22 – 01/01/23

Plans

☐ 26. MONDAY

☐ 27. TUESDAY

☐ 28. WEDNESDAY

☐ 29. THURSDAY

☐ 30. FRIDAY

☐ 31. SATURDAY

☐ 1. SUNDAY

Must be done this week

If I have time

Calls and emails

Notes

BIRTHDAYS & IMPORTANT DATES

BIRTHDAYS & IMPORTANT DATES

Notes

Notes

Notes

Notes

Notes

Notes

Notes

Notes

Notes

Notes

Printed in Great Britain
by Amazon